HOW TO PLAY GOLF

Fundamentals Of Playing Golf, Golf Rules, Etiquette, Clubs, Balls, Types Of Play, & A Practice Schedule.. Be A Professional Golfer

LOOKMAN JOSIAH

Table of Contents

CHAPTER ONE 3

   INTRODUCTION..3

CHAPTER TWO 12

   CHOOSING THE RIGHT BALL........................12

   LEARNING TO PLAY 13

CHAPTER THREE 23

   BASIC SHOTS YOU SHOULD KNOW 23

   THANK YOU..30

CHAPTER ONE

INTRODUCTION

Golf can seem extraordinarily complicated to the uninitiated. So many rules, so many one-of-a-kind sorts of clubs. And then there's the lingo: birdies, bogeys, bump-and-runs. At Golf Digest, this will be the language we speak every day, however we also understand it's a language which can scare prospective golfers off earlier than they ever choose up a membership. That are this online amateur's guide is available in. To folks that know nothing approximately golf, our intention is to shepherd you via this uncertainty. What form of clubs do you want? How do you practice? When do you understand which you're geared up for the golfing path? The way we see it, the best dumb questions about getting began in golfing are those you are afraid to invite, or worse, the ones for which you can't find a solution.

WHAT YOU NEED TO KNOW ABOUT CLUBS

No doubt, the proper device constantly enables, however it's not as though you may need to empty your savings account to get commenced. Instead, consciousness on locating the sort of system so as to allow you to broaden your imperfect skills with minimum expense. There'll be masses of time to head after the latest, warm merchandise on the market (and whilst you do, make certain you begin your seek with considered one of our top a hundred club fitters, but at the beginning, make studying -- and not buying -- your priority.

1. You only need a few golf equipment: You're allowed to carry as many as 14 golf equipment on your bag, however you may not need almost that many when you're first gaining knowledge of. Instead, begin with a motive force, a putter, a sand wedge (it's the membership that has an "S" on the sole or a loft of fifty four to fifty six levels) and complement those with

a 6-iron, an 8-iron, a pitching wedge, and a fairway wood or hybrid with 18-21 levels of loft. These are the golf equipment which can be the most forgiving and simplest to get airborne. You can find used and new titanium drivers for as low as $75 and putters for lots much less as on line, however most large golfing and widespread sporting items stoes additionally offer racks of discounted and/or used golf equipment.

2.   Don't guess -- strive earlier than you purchase: If you're an absolute newbie searching to shop for clubs, go to a bigger golf keep or driving variety and ask to attempt a 6-iron with a ordinary-flex and a stiff-flex shaft. (Generally, the faster and greater competitive the swing, the more you may pick a shaft that is categorized "S" for stiff.) One of the 2 needs to sense simpler to control. That's the shaft flex you need to start with for all of your clubs. Once you get extreme approximately the game and are

capable of make regular touch, a club fitting will permit you to get the most out of your gadget.

3. The more loft, the better: Unless you're a strong and nicely-coordinated athlete experienced with stick and ball sports (baseball, softball, hockey, tennis, for instance), choose woods which have greater loft. Why? The extra loft normally way it'll be easier to get the ball in the air and can also lessen sidespin so pictures fly straighter. So pass for drivers with at the least 10 degrees of loft and

fairway woods that start at 17 stages, now not 15 levels.

Four. Take gain of clubs made for novices: Some forms of clubs are easier to hit than others. For one factor, you're better off with hybrids as opposed to three-, 4-, and five-irons. And irons with wider soles (the bottom a part of an iron) will alleviate the tendency for the membership to stick inside the ground when you hit to a ways behind the ball. Also, with more weight focused in the sole, the iron's center of gravity can be decrease and this will assist photographs release on a higher trajectory. Generally, a extra forgiving iron will feature a sole that measures approximately the width of two fingers (from front aspect to again). If an iron's sole measures less than one finger width, you only should be gambling it if you're paid to achieve this. To locate the proper iron for you, browse via the splendid game improvement irons on our Hot List.

CHAPTER TWO

CHOOSING THE RIGHT BALL

Buy balls on a sliding scale primarily based on how many you lose in a spherical. If you've never played earlier than or lose sleeves or more a round, purchase balls that price around $20 a dozen (if you cannot determine between one emblem over another, strive setting some to peer how they sense coming off the putter face). When you chop the quantity of lost balls lower back to perhaps 3 to five balls a round, buy balls that price less than $30 a dozen. Only in case you're dropping less than a sleeve a spherical ought to you recall the $40 a dozen balls. For a whole rundown of golfing balls, see our ball Hot List.

LEARNING TO PLAY

The hardest element about golfing can be getting started out. Ask yourself some questions. First, why do you need to play? Is it for paintings or social motives? Maybe then you definitely want only a few primary instruction and patient friends. Perhaps you're seeking to soar in headfirst in hopes of having better rapid. If so, there may be lots of pinnacle-level preparation accessible. Next, how a good deal are you inclined to place into it? That goes for time and the cash. Point is, there is a huge difference between trying to experience around and have some laughs and being a serious participant. Do a few soul-looking, and begin to increase your plan.

1. Take instructions proper away: The terrible information

when you're simply starting out is you don't know a lot about golfing. The proper news? You do not know a great deal about golfing. You probably have not ingrained many horrific habits, and you've got tons of questions on what to do. Nothing beats beginning out with a few fine courses. And do not simply are trying to find preparation while you're suffering. It's simply as essential to recognize what you're doing proper as what you are doing wrong. Your golf buddies would possibly once in a while have an excellent tip for you, but it is higher to are searching for out a PGA expert given that they are the ones educated to teach the game to someone like yourself. To discover a first rate trainer close to you.

2. Have a variety habitual: Everyone desires to see how a ways they could hit a golf ball, but while you go to the driving variety, withstand the temptation to at once begin ripping drivers. Yes, you would possibly crank a pair, however swinging for maximum distance will throw you out of sync

-- and fast. Start out via hitting one in every of your wedges or quick irons, warming up your golf muscular tissues with 1/2-swings. Then boom the length and speed of your swings, and flow on for your middle irons. Work your way up to the driving force, and once you hit a few balls with it, move back to a quick iron or wedge. This will assist you preserve your tempo and tension stage in test.

3.   Learn the short photographs: Roughly half of your strokes come within   50   yards   of   the

inexperienced. That approach you probably should spend half of of your exercise time together with your wedges and putter. This would possibly sound dull, but the correct news is, you can practice your short recreation for your very own back yard -- even on your TV room. Put out some buckets on your backyard at diverse distances and try and pitch balls into them. Give yourself right lies and bad lies, similar to you get at the path. As for placing, your carpet won't play as fast because the greens, but you may nevertheless exercise aiming and rolling balls thru doors and into furniture legs.

4.   When doubtful, move lower back to fundamentals: Golf can surely get you wondering too much.   There's   plenty   of information accessible, and the maximum thoughts-numbing part can be the practice. When you are a new golfer, you can't help but examine it and watch it, however too much can be, nicely, too much. When you locate yourself getting burned out from an excessive amount of swing questioning, pass

returned to fundamentals. Try to get yourself into an amazing setup -- check your ball position and posture -- then make a at ease swing all the manner to a full end. Over-wondering creates anxiety, so be aware about your pressure stage: Waggle the membership a touch at deal with and try to make a easy circulate off the ball. Nothing ruins your chances quicker than snatching the membership returned.

5. Find the right instructor: Finding an trainer you believe can

truly pace your development. Of route you want your trainer to be knowledgeable and committed to assisting you, but simply as critical is finding an excellent personality suit. If you are laid returned, you might like a teacher with a low-key technique. If you're a innovative kind, you might paintings satisfactory with someone who teaches with feels and pix as opposed to angles and positions. The point is, you want to be comfortable and revel in the experience. You'll study first-class when you sense loose to ask what you observed are stupid questions

and whilst you're no longer afraid

to cave in a few times.

CHAPTER THREE

BASIC SHOTS YOU SHOULD KNOW

There are components of golfing as a way to elude you your whole existence, but certain fundamentals are crucial. You have as a way to hit a motive force off the tee with a fair amount of self assurance. You have a good way to hit an iron off the floor, and get out of a greenside bunker. You ought to recognize some basic brief photographs across the inexperienced, and be capable of keep your cool when matters get unsightly.

1.   Know whilst to chip and while to pitch: When you have a quick shot to the inexperienced, you're going to hit both a chip and a pitch. What's the distinction among the two? A chip shot stays low and runs alongside the floor, and a pitch flies higher and doesn't roll as a great deal. Use a chip when you don't ought to deliver the ball over an obstacle, like deep hard or a bunker, and you've a number of inexperienced between

you and the hole. Use a pitch if you have to carry over something or want to forestall the ball quicker. The more peak on a pitch shot reasons the ball to land softer and stop faster.

2.   Get out of a bunker on every occasion: The greenside bunker shot is the only shot in golfing where you don't sincerely hit the ball: You swing the club head into the sand at the back of the ball, and the sand pushes it out. For that reason, you have to swing pretty a chunk more difficult than

you would possibly count on; the sand without a doubt slows down the club head. Here's the fundamental technique: Using your sand wedge, stand so the ball is even along with your front instep, twist your toes in for stability, and awareness on a gap approximately inches in the back of the ball. Swing the membership returned about halfway then down and through that spot at the back of the ball. Keep turning your body so your chest faces the goal at the finish.

3. Use your athleticism: Beginning golfers regularly get so tied up within the instructions for making the swing that they lose their athletic instincts. Golf might be greater mental than different sports; however the swing continues to be a dynamic, athletic motion. Here are some sports activities photos that will help you: At address, stand like a defender in basketball, along with your legs lively and your weight balanced left to right and front to returned. On the backswing, think about a quarterback rearing returned to

make a skip: Arm stretched lower back and body coiled from top to bottom. And at the downswing, be like a hockey participant hitting a slap shot, along with your wrists staying firm and your arms main the clubhead into the ball.

So now which you've were given a few golf equipment and you've got discovered the basics of the golf swing, you are considering trying out yourself on an actual golfing direction. Great, however it is no longer as in case you must step right onto the identical direction the professionals play. If you need to make sure your early experiences on the golf path are nice ones, it is nice to realize your barriers, and then build yourself up.

THANK YOU.